# SPORTS

Kay Robertson

rourkeeducationalmedia.com

Scan for Related Titles
and Teacher Resources

www.rourkeeducationalmedia.com

PHOTO CREDITS: Cover (top) © imging, (main) © Susan Leggett; back cover, © Brian Gudas – 1; © miflippo, 4; © xjben, 5; © PILart, 6; © Pgiam, 7; © Everett Collection, 8; © Lawrence Weslowski Jr, , Creative Commons, XXX Sports - Baseball, 9; © JSABBOTT, 10; © James Boardman | Dreamstime.com, 11; ©      jgareri, 12; © Stephen Mcsweeny, 13; © Matt_Brown, 14; © Daniel M. Silva / Shutterstock.com, 15; © Willierossin, 16; © Willierossin, 17; © Seregal, 18; © Stephen Coburn, Creative Commons, 19; © RTimages,  20; © filo, Creative Commons, 21; © filo, Creative Commons, 22; © Flashon Studio, 23; © Jerry Coli | Dreamstime.com, 24; © filo, 25; © Vasily Smirnov / Shutterstock.com, 27; © esolla, Pavel L Photo and Video / Shutterstock.com, 28; © joyfull / Shutterstock.com, 29; © melhi, imagedepotpro,     yesfoto, 315 studio , 30; © Kevin Norris / Shutterstock.com, Action Sports Photography / Shutterstock.com, 31, ; © Action Sports Photography / Shutterstock.com, Vladru, 32; © EPG_EuroPhotoGraphics / Shutterstock.com, 33; © EPG_EuroPhotoGraphics / Shutterstock.com, Doug James / Shutterstock.com,  34; © Action Sports Photography / Shutterstock.com, 35; © Beelde Photography / shutterstock.com, 36; © luciana ellington, 37; © Featureflash / Shutterstock.com, 38; © filibuster, 39; © XXX, 40; © A. Einsiedler / Shutterstock.com, 41; © Charles Knox, 42; © S.Pytel, XXX, monkeybusinessimages, 43; © Maxim Petrichuk / Shutterstock.com, Yuri Kravchenko / Shutterstock.com, 44; © Lokibaho

Edited by: Jill Sherman

Cover design by: Nicola Stratford, bdpublishing.com

Interior design by: Cory Davis

**Library of Congress PCN Data**

STEM Guides to Sports / Kay Robertson.
     p. cm. --  (STEM Everyday)
Includes index.
ISBN 978-1-62169-847-0 (hardcover)
ISBN 978-1-62169-742-8 (softcover)
ISBN 978-1-62169-950-7 (e-Book)
Library of Congress Control Number:  2013936452

**Also Available as:**

Rourke Educational Media
Printed in the United States of America,
North Mankato, Minnesota

Rourke

rourkeeducationalmedia.com
customerservice@rourkeeducationalmedia.com • PO Box 643328 Vero Beach, Florida 32964

# TABLE OF CONTENTS

# INTRODUCTION

Do athletes and coaches use math? Can you play sports without doing math?

Well, for one thing, mathematics plays a large part in how winning is determined.

But in the relationship between math and sports, scores are just the tip of the iceberg. In fact, it wouldn't be unreasonable to say that sports are pure math. Mathematics in motion!

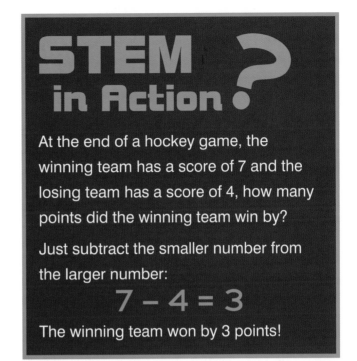

# STEM in Action?

At the end of a hockey game, the winning team has a score of 7 and the losing team has a score of 4, how many points did the winning team win by?

Just subtract the smaller number from the larger number:

$$7 - 4 = 3$$

The winning team won by 3 points!

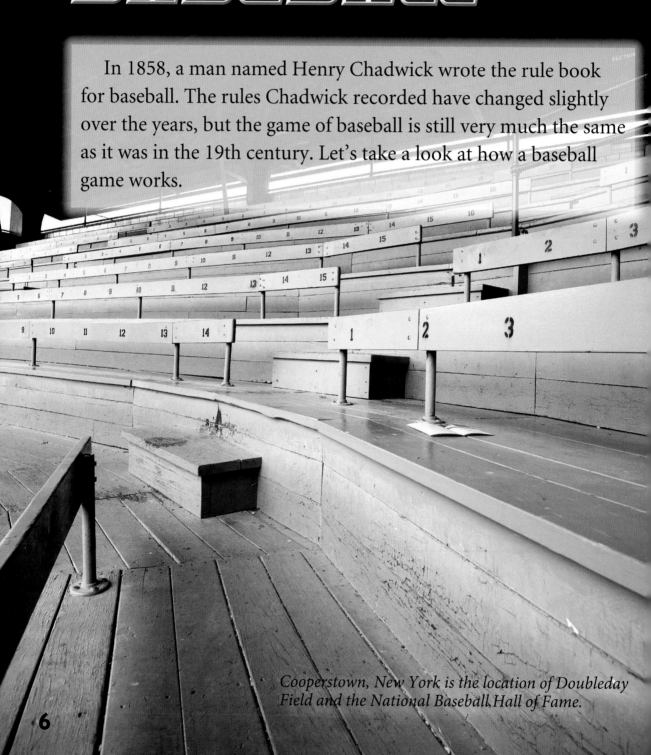

# MATH IN BASEBALL

In 1858, a man named Henry Chadwick wrote the rule book for baseball. The rules Chadwick recorded have changed slightly over the years, but the game of baseball is still very much the same as it was in the 19th century. Let's take a look at how a baseball game works.

*Cooperstown, New York is the location of Doubleday Field and the National Baseball Hall of Fame.*

# STEM in Action?

It is believed that the first game of modern baseball was played in 1845 in Hoboken, New Jersey. Using that date as a starting point, can you figure out how old baseball is?

Let's assume that the year you are reading this book is 2014. Now all you have to do to find the answer is to subtract the smaller number from the larger number:

$$2014 - 1845 = 169$$

Baseball is about 169 years old!

In a baseball game, there are two teams. These teams take turns playing **offense** and **defense**. The team playing defense has 9 players on the field in the following postitions: pitcher, catcher, first baseman, second baseman, third baseman, shortstop, right fielder, center fielder, left fielder.

Meanwhile, the team playing offense sends batters to home plate. The batters attempt to hit the balls thrown by the pitcher to the catcher. The distance from the pitcher's mound to home plate is 60.5 feet (18.44 meters).

Professional pitchers are capable of throwing a baseball at incredible speeds. Much of the time, these pitches reach velocities of over 90 miles per hour (145 kilometers per hour)!

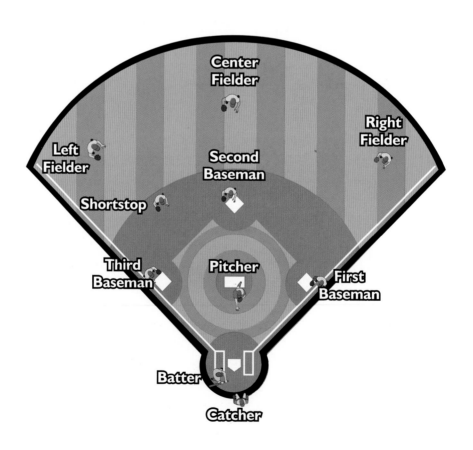

*If this boy delivers a pitch that travels at 60 miles per hour (97 kilometers per hour), how quickly will it reach the batter?*

# STEM in Action?

If a baseball is traveling at 90 mph, how long does it take to travel 60.5 feet?

It is important to understand that we are comparing a very large value (the speed of the ball) to a much smaller value (the distance from the pitcher's mound to home plate). In order to calculate a sensible answer, you're going to have to convert some numbers.

In one mile, there are 5,280 feet. How many feet are there in 90 miles?

$$90 \times 5{,}280 = 475{,}200$$

So a baseball traveling at 90 mph is traveling at 475,200 feet per hour!

As you can imagine, a baseball traveling at that speed won't take very long to reach the catcher's mitt. In fact, it's pointless to talk about it in terms of a measurement per hour. Rather, a baseball traveling at that speed will reach home plate in a matter of seconds.

# STEM in Action?

How many seconds are there in one hour? There are 60 minutes in an hour, and 60 seconds per minute, so:

$$60 \times 60 = 3{,}600$$

There are 3,600 seconds in one hour!

If a baseball is traveling at 475,200 feet per hour, how many feet is it covering per second? You can find out by dividing the speed of the baseball per hour by the number of seconds in an hour:

$$475{,}200 \div 3{,}600 = 132$$

The baseball is traveling at a speed of 132 feet per second! How long will it take a ball traveling at that speed to go 60.5 feet from the pitcher's mound to home plate?

You can find out by dividing the distance by the speed:

$$60.5 \div 132 = 0.4583$$

A ball thrown at 90 miles per hour reaches home plate in less than half a second!

*If this boy ends the season with 400 at-bats and 57 hits, what is his batting average?*

Baseballs traveling at incredibly high speeds can be dangerous. The catcher always wears a protective mask and catches with a mitt.

Batting averages are determined using two numbers. The first is the number of times at-bat, or the number of chances a player has to hit a ball. The second number is the number of actual hits a player gets.

Another way to think about this is to consider the batting average in terms of percentage. A batting **average** is really a number that tells what percentage of balls a player has managed to hit.

What is a good batting average? Anything over .270 is considered good, while an average over .300 is great. Anything over .330 is incredible.

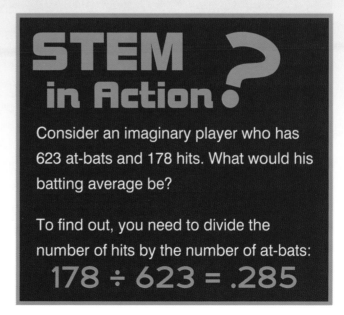

# STEM in Action?

Consider an imaginary player who has 623 at-bats and 178 hits. What would his batting average be?

To find out, you need to divide the number of hits by the number of at-bats:

$$178 \div 623 = .285$$

# STEM in Action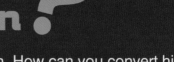

Let's take a look at the imaginary player again. How can you convert his batting average of .285 to a percentage?

It's easy. Just multiply it by 100:

$$.285 \times 100 = 28.5$$

He hit 28.5 percent! That wouldn't be a very good test score, but it's considered good for a batter. That gives you some idea of just how hard it is to hit a baseball coming at you at 90 miles per hour!

# STEM Fast Fact

*Bary Bonds hitting a home run.*

**Home Run Kings**

For forty years, the baseball player responsible for hitting the most home runs in a single season was Roger Maris. In 1961, Maris hit a total of 61 home runs, narrowly outdoing the previous record of 60 set by Babe Ruth. In 1998, this record was beaten twice by Mark McGwire of the St. Louis Cardinals and Sammy Sosa of the Chicago Cubs. Their totals were 70 home runs for McGwire and 66 for Sosa. The current record, though, is held by Barry Bonds, who in 2001 managed to hit 73 home runs!

*How many more home runs did Barry Bonds get than Roger Maris?*

$$73 - 61 = 12$$

*Bonds got 12 more home runs than Maris!*

# MATH IN FOOTBALL

Baseball is unique in that it is played on a diamond-shaped field. But most sports, including soccer, hockey, and lacrosse, are played on rectangular fields. Probably the most popular American sport played on a rectangular field is football.

*Including the end zones, a football field is 120 yards (109.73 meters) long. How long is half of a football field including the end zone?*

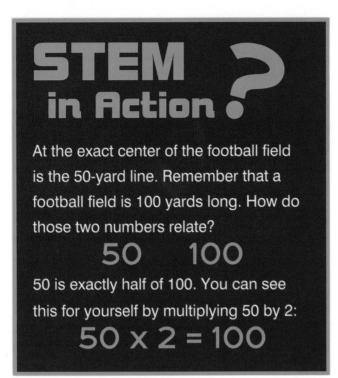
Without counting the end zones, which take up a space of 10 yards (9.14 meters) each, a professional football field is exactly 100 yards (91.44 meters) long. Football fields are labeled with a series of yard lines.

This is an important point to make in terms of understanding how football is played. A football field is like two separate fields stuck together. The team with possession of the ball (the offense) tries to invade the defending team's field and eventually cross their goal line to score a touchdown. Starting from the 50-yard line, a team on the offense has to push forward 50 yards to get a touchdown.

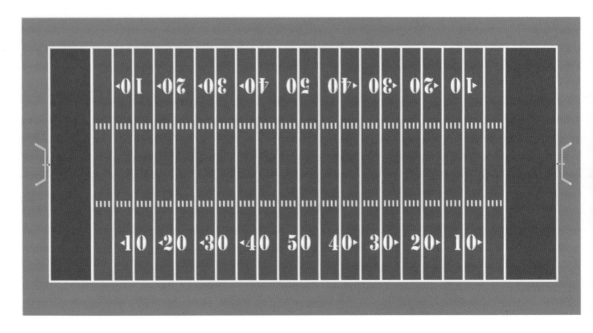

The defense tries to prevent the offensive team from gaining yardage by pushing the **line of scrimmage** back. The line of scrimmage is a set of imaginary lines that determine where players will line up before the next play, and its location is determined by where the last play ended.

## STEM in Action?

What if the defense manages to push the offensive line from the 50-yard line to the 30-yard line? How many yards does the offense now have to cover to make a touchdown?

First of all, you have to find out how many yards away from the 50-yard line the offense is. You can do this by subtracting the team's current location from 50:

$$50 - 30 = 20$$

The offense team is 20 yards from the 50-yard line!

Now add the two remaining distances together:

$$50 + 20 = 70$$

To make a touchdown, the offense team has to cover 70 yards!

The team that has possession of the ball is given just 4 downs, or plays, to move the ball forward 10 yards (9.14 meters). If the offense fails to do this, the ball is given to the other side.

## STEM in Action?

Imagine that the offense advances the ball by 4 yards on the first down. How many yards does it have to go?

$$10 - 4 = 6$$

6 yards!

But what if the defense pushes the offense back 7 yards? How many yards do they have to move forward after that?

$$10 + 7 = 17$$

17 yards!

*A professional football team can have up to 53 players, but only 11 of those players are allowed on the field at any time.*

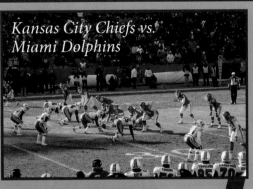

*Kansas City Chiefs vs. Miami Dolphins*

# STEM Fast Fact!

### The Longest Game

A football game is made up of 4 quarters lasting 15 minutes each. How long is that in total?

$$4 \times 15 = 60$$

60 minutes, or one hour!

But this total doesn't take time-outs or overtime into account. Overtime is necessary if the score is tied. In order to break the tie, they have to keep playing. The longest game in NFL history took place in 1971 between the Kansas City Chiefs and the Miami Dolphins. It lasted 82 minutes. How much longer than a standard game is that?

$$82 - 60 = 22$$

22 minutes!

*What Americans call soccer is known in most of the world as football, and our football is called American football.*

# MATH IN BASKETBALL

Basketball is another sport that uses a rectangular field of play. A regulation NBA basketball court is 94 feet (28.65 meters) long and 50 feet (15.24 meters) wide. At either end of the court are baskets mounted onto a backboard precisely 10 feet (3.05 meters) off the ground.

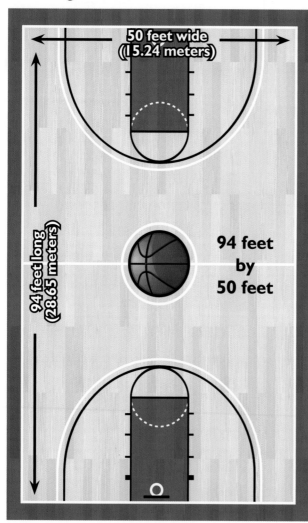

*The surface of a basketball court is made of highly polished wood, usually maple.*

If you watch a professional basketball game on television, you'll notice that both teams have many players. This allows for substitutions. Each team can have up to five players on the court an any given time. These players cover the following positions:

1. **Point guard**
2. **Shooting guard**
3. **Power forward**
4. **Small forward**
5. **Center**

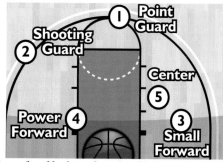

In comparison with baseball and football, basketball is a much quicker game. Both teams score points at a fast rate. This is partly why the point totals of basketball games are so high, sometimes even going into triple-digit numbers.

# STEM in Action?

How tall are you? Imagine for a moment, that you are four and a half feet tall. How much higher up is the basket on a basketball court?

$$10 - 4.5 = 5.5$$

The basket on a basketball court is five and a half feet higher than you are! Now you understand why most basketball players are very tall!

Assuming that both teams in a basketball game have as many players on the court as allowed, how many players in total are on the court?

$$5 + 5 = 10$$

10 players!

# STEM in Action?

Can you calculate the average total points per game for the top ten point leaders?

It's easy to do. First, add up all of the totals:

$$30.1 + 30.1 + 27.6 + 27.4 + 27.0 + 26.7 + 26.4 + 26.4 + 26.2 + 25.7 = 273.6$$

Next, divide the total by the number of **addends**. Addends are the numbers you added together. Since you already know that these are the numbers for ten players, you know that there are 10 addends:

$$273.6 \div 10 = 27.36$$

The average score for the top ten leaders in points per game is 27.36!

*What is your average total points per basketball game?*

In high-scoring games, individual players may be responsible for a lot of the points scored.

Here is a chart showing the ten all-time leaders for points per game:

| Player | Total |
| --- | --- |
| Michael Jordan | 30.1 |
| Wilt Chamberlain | 30.1 |
| LeBron James | 27.6 |
| Elgin Baylor | 27.4 |
| Jerry West | 27.0 |
| Allen Iverson | 26.7 |
| Kevin Durant | 26.4 |
| Bob Pettit | 26.4 |
| George Gervin | 26.2 |
| Oscar Robertson | 25.7 |

Something to bear in mind when looking at this chart is that it shows the **average** number of points scored per game. An average is a number that represents a group of numbers. In other words, Bob Pettit didn't earn 26.4 points for every game he played, but 26.4 is about the number of points he earned in most games.

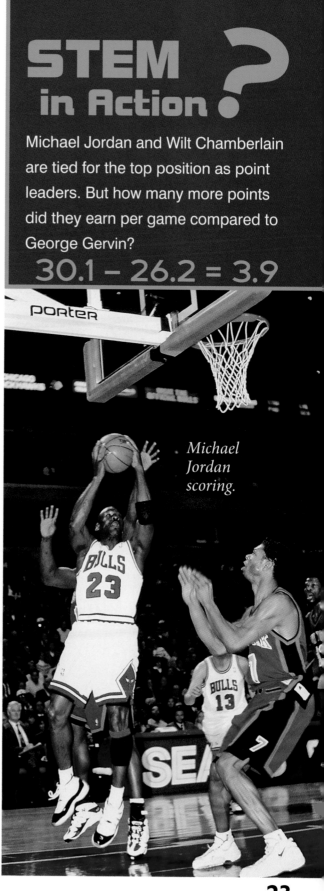

# STEM in Action ?

Michael Jordan and Wilt Chamberlain are tied for the top position as point leaders. But how many more points did they earn per game compared to George Gervin?

$$30.1 - 26.2 = 3.9$$

*Michael Jordan scoring.*

# STEM
## Fast Fact!

**Basketball Scoring**

Each basket in a game of basketball can be worth anything from 1 point up to 3 points. It all depends on where the basket was shot:

**From behind the three-point line = 3 points**

**From inside the three-point line = 2 points**

**Foul shot = 1 point**

So, if a player in a basketball game makes 7 baskets from inside the three-point line, 2 baskets from behind the three-point line, and 1 foul shot, how many points has he or she earned?

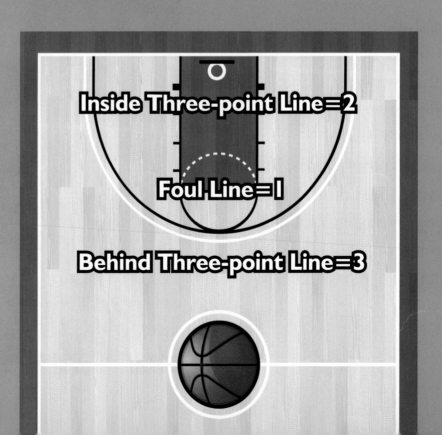

Inside Three-point Line=2

Foul Line=1

Behind Three-point Line=3

# MATH IN BOXING

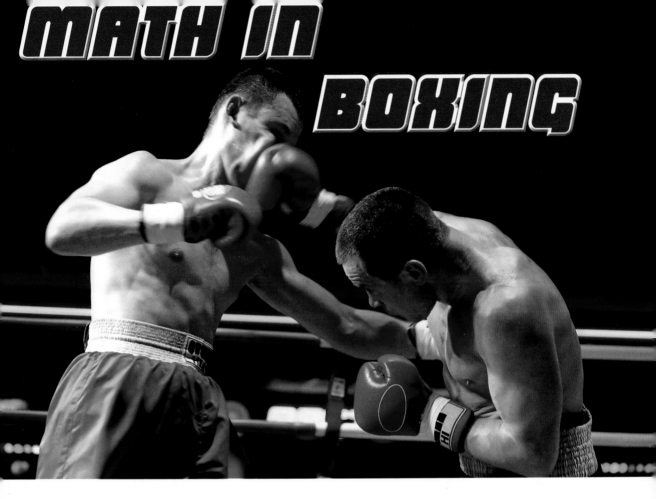

Not all sports involve large teams or a great deal of equipment. One of the oldest sports is also one of the simplest, boxing.

Boxing dates as far back as ancient Egypt, making it roughly 4,000 years old. Of course, the boxing we are familiar with today is very different from the boxing that was practiced by the Egyptians and later by the Greeks. For one thing, boxers in ancient times did not wear gloves. Another important difference is that modern boxing has weight categories.

You may already know something about weight classes even if you don't realize. Who is the most famous boxer in the world? Mike Tyson is famous for being the youngest person to ever win the heavyweight title.

Lightweight, middleweight, heavyweight… These are all distinctions made to ensure fairness. It wouldn't be very fair for a small person to fight a much larger person. The larger person would have an unfair advantage. In order to prevent a situation like this, boxers are categorized according to how much they weigh. These categories are called weight divisions.

# STEM Fast Fact !

According to the World Boxing Council, there are seventeen weight divisions:

| | |
|---|---|
| Strawweight | 105 pounds |
| Lightflyweight | 108 pounds |
| Flyweight | 112 pounds |
| Super Flyweight | 115 pounds |
| Bantamweight | 118 pounds |
| Superbantamweight | 122 pounds |
| Featherweight | 126 pounds |
| Superfeatherweight | 130 pounds |
| Lightweight | 135 pounds |
| Superlightweight | 140 pounds |
| Welterweight | 147 pounds |
| Superwelterweight | 154 pounds |
| Middleweight | 160 pounds |
| Supermiddleweight | 168 pounds |
| Lightheavyweight | 175 pounds |
| Cruiserweight | 200 pounds |
| Heavyweight | over 200 pounds with no upper limit |

Each weight division is defined by a top limit in each category. For instance, in order to qualify as a featherweight, a boxer can weigh anywhere between 123 and 126 pounds (55.8 to 57.1 kilograms). Anything over that would place the boxer in the next category, superfeatherweight.

# STEM in Action?

Figure out how many more pounds a flyweight boxer weighs compared to a strawweight boxer.

To find out, just subtract the smaller number from the larger number:

$$112 - 105 = 7$$

A flyweight boxer weighs about 7 pounds more than a strawweight boxer!

What about a lightweight boxer compared to a super flyweight boxer?

$$135 - 115 = 20$$

A lightweight boxer weighs about 20 pounds more than a super flyweight boxer!

*How much do you weigh? How much more would you need to weigh to qualify as a heavyweight?*

# STEM in Action ?

The heaviest category, the heavyweight division, has no upper weight limit. If you had two boxers with these weights:

315                 225

They would both qualify as heavyweights! How many more pounds is 315 compared to 225?

$$315 - 225 = 90$$

The boxer weighing 315 is 90 pounds heavier than the boxer weighing 225! And yet they are both still in the heavyweight division!

Compare a heavyweight boxer weighing 215 pounds to someone in the lightest category, a strawweight:

$$215 - 105 = 110$$

A 215 pound heavyweight boxer weighs about 110 pounds more than a strawweight boxer. Now you can see why weight divisions are necessary for a fair fight.

# STEM
## Fast Fact

**The Olympics**

Baseball, basketball, and boxing are just some of the many games that make up the Olympics, a festival of sports that originated in Greece many hundreds of years ago. Other sports in the Olympics include tennis, volleyball, and fencing among many, many others.

Ever since the 1992 Olympics, the games have been held in two-year intervals, alternating the Summer and Winter games. For example, the Winter games were held in 1994. Then, two years later, in 1996, they had the Summer Olympics.

The Summer Olympics were held in 2012. Which year will the Summer Olympics be held again?

## 1996, 2000, 2004, 2008, 2012, ????

# MATH IN NASCAR

Many of the sports we have been looking at are things you would not likely experience unless you played them. There is one sport, though, that almost everyone can relate to on some level, simply because it is such a common part of everyday life.

Driving is something that almost everyone will experience at one point or another. But the driving that NASCAR drivers do is much different than the driving you see people do in your neighborhood. NASCAR drivers race on specially paved tracks at extremely high speeds. Most of the time these speeds are well over 200 miles per hour (322 kilometers per hour).

NASCAR is actually an **acronym**, a word made from the first letters in a group of words. NASCAR comes from the National Association of Stock Car Racing.

NASCAR has only been in existence for a little over 50 years, but since that time it has become an immensely popular sport. Crowds all over the country can't get enough of the speeding, roaring cars.

*In NASCAR a checkered flag means the race is finished.*

# STEM in Action

Let's compare NASCAR speeds to the speed limit in a typical residential neighborhood, about 30 miles per hour.

### 200          30

To see how much faster a NASCAR diver is, subtract 30 from 200:

## 200 – 30 = 170

That gives you 170. So a NASCAR driver travels at an average speed of 170 miles per hour faster than a person driving through a residential neighborhood!

# STEM in Action?

Another way to think about this, though, is to express the difference in terms of multiples. It might help you to think of the word multiples as being related to multiplication. You see, any number being multiplied produces multiples.

Let's apply this technique to the speeds of an everyday driver and a NASCAR driver:

$$200 \div 30 = 6.66$$

And just to keep things simple, round that number up to 7. Now you can say that a NASCAR driver drives at speeds about seven times as fast as an everyday driver!

$$0 \times 7 = 0 \qquad 1 \times 7 = 7 \qquad 2 \times 7 = 14$$

The answers 0, 7, and 14 are all multiples of 7!

Now consider these numbers:

$$5 \qquad\qquad 10$$

What would you have to multiply the number 5 by to give the product 10? You can find out by using division:

$$10 \div 5 = 2$$

Multiplying 5 by 2 equals 10. Another thing you can say here, though, is that the product 10 is twice as much as 5!

# STEM
## Fast Fact!

**The Longest Track**

The longest race in NASCAR is the Coca-Cola 600. The number 600 refers to the number of miles in the race. If a typical car in the Coca-Cola 600 is traveling at 200 miles per hour, how long will it take that car to complete a 600-mile distance?

$$600 \div 200 = 3$$

3 hours!

# MATH IN SKATEBOARDING

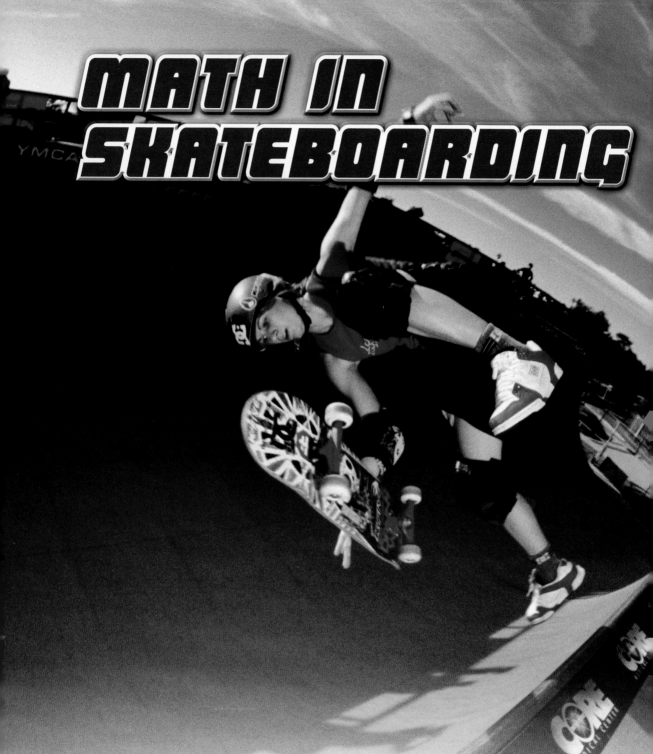

Just riding around on a skateboard without wiping out takes a lot of practice. That is why all the flashy tricks performed by professional skateboarders are so impressive. The ollie, the manual, and grinding all take fantastic coordination and skill.

*Before it was known as skateboarding it was called sidewalk surfing!*

Probably the most famous skateboarder of all time is Tony Hawk. One of Tony's biggest achievements came at the 1999 X Games when he became the first person ever to perform a stunt many thought was impossible. This stunt is called the 900. It took Hawk about 10 years of practice before he was able to do it successfully.

In a 900, a skater launches from a U-shaped skating ramp. While airborne, he rotates two and a half times. To understand why this trick is called a 900, you have to understand a bit about circles and degrees.

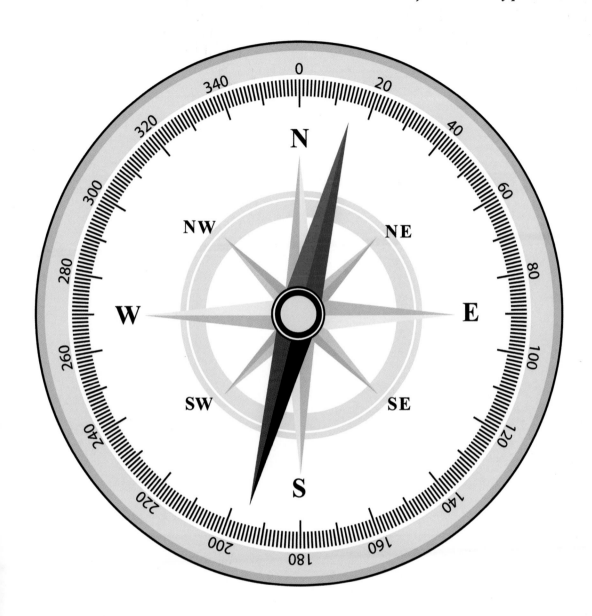

Degrees are a unit of measurement for circles developed by the ancient Greeks. A degree is basically a very small portion of a circle, like thin slices of a pie. Every circle can be divided into 360 degrees. It might help you to understand this concept better by looking closely at a compass. A compass is a circle marked with clearly labeled degrees. The starting point of a circle is 0 degrees. One complete revolution is 360 degrees.

**39**

# STEM in Action?

To perform a 900, a skateboarder has to rotate two and a half times. How many degrees is that?

First of all, find out how many degrees there are in two revolutions:

$$2 \times 360 = 720$$

There are 720 degrees in two revolutions!

Now you have to find out how many degrees there are in half a revolution. You already know that there are 360 degrees in one full revolution. You can find out how many degrees there are in half a revolution by dividing that amount by 2:

$$360 \div 2 = 180$$

There are 180 degrees in half a revolution!

To find out how many degrees there are in two and a half revolutions, you just have to add the results together:

$$720 + 180 = 900$$

There are 900 degrees in two and a half revolutions! Now you know where the trick gets its name!

*Skate parks have built-in ramps that will help you practice and develop your own tricks.*

# STEM
# Fast Fact !

**Longboards**

Typical skateboards are about 31 inches long.But some skateboarders want to go faster than a skateboard can travel. At that point, they can switch to something called a longboard.

The average longboard can be anywhere from 38 to 60 inches long.

If you have a longboard that is 45 inches long, how much longer is that than the average skateboard?

$$45 - 31 = 14$$

Fourteen inches longer!

# CONCLUSION

What is your favorite sport? Maybe you have more than one. Certainly, there is a wide variety to choose from. If you don't like playing tennis you may like swimming. You may not like running, but maybe you enjoy skiing. Even people who don't actually play sports like to watch games and root for their favorite teams.

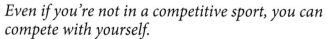
*Even if you're not in a competitive sport, you can compete with yourself.*

*There are many sports to choose from.*

In this book we've mostly looked at competitive sports, or sports that people play to earn points and win at something. There is another kind of sports that has more to do with enjoyment and fun. These are called **recreational** sports. Even recreational sports are full of math. How fast you go, how far you go, how long you do it, numbers are what we use to measure all of these things. Sometimes, even if you're not competing with other people, you are in competition with yourself. Many runners, for instance, keep records to see how much they improve from week to week and month to month.

Did you know that there are even competitions where young people solve math problems? That means that not only is math a part of sports, it is a sport! Maybe you'll even want to try it for yourself!

# GLOSSARY

**acronym** (AK-ruh-nim): a word made from the first letters of other words

**addends** (AD-ends): the numbers added together in an addition problem

**average** (AV-ur-ij): a number used to represent a group of numbers

**defense** (DEE-fens): the team trying to prevent the offense from scoring

**line of scrimmage** (line uhv SKRIM-ij): in football, the location on the field where play begins

**offense** (AW-fens): the team in possession of the ball

**recreational** (rek-ree-AY-shuhn-uhl): for fun and enjoyment

# INDEX

# METRIC SYSTEM

We actually have two systems of weights and measures in the United States. Quarts, pints, gallons, ounces, and pounds are all units of the U.S. Customary System, also known as the English System.

The other system of measurement, and the only one sanctioned by the United States Government, is the metric system, which is also known as the International System of Units. French scientists developed the metric system in the 1790s. The basic unit of measurement in the metric system is the meter, which is about one ten-millionth the distance from the North Pole to the equator.

For practice, you could go through this book and convert some of the numbers to metric.

Try it!

| Converting Imperial to Metric | | | |
|---|---|---|---|
| Convert | To | Multiply by | Example |
| inches (in) | millimeters (mm) | 25.40 | 2in x 25.40 = 50.8mm |
| inches (in) | centimeters (cm) | 2.54 | 2in x 2.54 = 5.08cm |
| feet (ft) | meters (m) | 0.30 | 2ft x .30 = 0.6m |
| yards (yd) | meters (m) | 0.91 | 2yd x .91 = 1.82m |
| miles (mi) | kilometers (km) | 1.61 | 2mi x 1.61 = 3.22km |
| miles per hour (mph) | kilometers per hour (km/h) | 1.61 | 2mph x 1.61 = 3.22km/h |
| ounces (oz) | grams (g) | 28.35 | 2oz x 28.35 = 56.7g |
| pounds (lb) | kilograms (kg) | 0.454 | 2lb x .454 = 0.908kg |
| tons (T) | metric ton (MT) | 1.016 | 2T x 1.016 = 2.032 |
| ounces (oz) | milliliters (ml) | 29.57 | 2oz x 29.57 = 59.14ml |
| pint (pt) | liter (l) | 0.55 | 2pt x .55 = 1.1l |
| quarts (qt) | liters (l) | 0.95 | 2qt x .95 = 1.9l |
| gallons (gal) | liters (l) | 3.785 | 2gal x 3.785 = 7.57 |

# WEBSITES TO VISIT

www.pbs.org/teachersource/mathline/concepts/
  sportsandmathematics.shtm
PBS TeacherSource – Sports and Mathematics

people.howstuffworks.com/baseball.htm
How Stuff Works – How Baseball Works

www.acdelco.com/html/nas_main.htm
NACAR Basics

# SHOW WHAT YOU KNOW

1. How are points calculated in basketball?
2. If you scored a basket from a foul shot, how many points would you score?
3. Using the chart of the top ten leading point scorers in basketball, what is point difference between Elgin Baylor and Oscar Robertson?
4. Using the same chart, how many points would a player need to score to make it on this list? At the very top? At the very bottom?
5. Convert the distance between the pitcher's mound and home plate from feet to meters.